A CENTURY of
CHESTER

God's Providence House, early twentieth century.

A CENTURY of CHESTER

CLIFF HAYES

First published in the United Kingdom in 2001 by
Sutton Publishing Limited

This new paperback edition first published in 2012

The History Press
The Mill, Brimscombe Port
Stroud, Gloucestershire, GL5 2QG
www.thehistorypress.co.uk

British Library Cataloguing in Publication Data
A catalogue record for this book is available from the British Library.

ISBN 978-0-7524-7473-1

Illustrations

Front endpaper: The Chester Rows at the Cross, *c.* 1905.
Half title: Eastgate and the Victorian Jubilee Clock, *c.* 1950.
Title page: Greetings from Chester, 1928.
Back endpaper: The Cross at Chester, 2001.

The weir, walls and old Dee Bridge, 1950s.

Contents

Looking from Eastgate down the Shropshire Union Canal towards the River Dee. The first bridge in our photograph is known as the 'Bridge of Sighs', and was so named because prisoners waiting to be hanged were taken from the jail on the left of the bridge to the chapel of Little St John over on the right for one last prayer. When constructed at a cost of £20 in 1793 it had iron bars either side to stop the prisoners escaping. The canal was cut here at the site of the Roman defence moat.

Foreword

I t's a pleasure, privilege and real delight to write a foreword for this book – *A Century of Chester*. The current city was founded nearly 2,000 years ago, but remains a vibrant, friendly and human place. Chester is deeply loved by all those who live here, people who come here to work and our many guests who visit us.

The quality of life and historic fabric have been enhanced by many generations of talented architects, craftsmen and builders, and the work of the last hundred years has been no exception.

We attract over six million visitors from all over the globe every year. Both Chester Zoo – which is the one of the best in the world – and our cathedral, a site of Christian worship for two millennia, attract over a million each.

The historic medieval two-tier 'Rows' of shops, centred on the Cross, are unique.

Our racecourse, situated between the city walls and the river, is the oldest in the world and is recognised as a real gem.

Chester has long been known as the jewel in the crown of the North West of England, and I love it and its warm friendly citizenry with a passion. I am sure that everyone reading this book will enjoy and cherish that part of our city's story that it celebrates.

There's nowhere else I'd rather be.

Graham Proctor

Graham Syddall Proctor
former Lord Mayor of Chester

11

Chester's reinstated Cross as it looks today. Only the top of the cross is original. The original base is at Plas Newydd, the house of the Ladies of Llangollen. The cross in our picture was placed here in 1975.

The Making of Chester

Chester is where it is and what it is because of the Roman invasion of Britain and the River Dee. Some historians tell us of an ancient British town called Cearlleon (Carthleon) Vawr, the chief town of Venedocia (North Wales). This information is based on the writings of the monks at Chester, whose work was translated many years later. The site of Carthleon was where Chester is today, but all vestige of it was swept away when the Romans began developing their fortifications. This is a very likely scenario, but is still impossible to prove. I would be the first to admit that some of our scriptured brethren in the thirteenth and fourteenth centuries were a little fanciful and over-imaginative at times.

The Romans liked to develop their forts on rivers, usually where it was easiest to ford. On the River Lune we have Lancaster, on the Ribble we have Ribchester and on the Mersey we have Warrington. The Dee, because of the Roodeye and the Earls Eey at this point made it an ideal place to build their fortifications. Ships could also sail right up to

Bridge Street from an 1850 drawing.

13

Chester as it was still tidal at the time, and this enabled the Romans to bring in men and materials easily.

The Roman army began arriving sometime in the middle of the first century, roughly AD 60 and at first constructed a ditch and earth defence to protect the wooden walls of their camp. These were soon replaced by stone walls, in around AD 90, with four porta (gates), named Principalis Dextra, Principalis Sinistra, Praetoria and Decumana. The building work would have gone on for over a century because towers were added to the walls, each tower a bow shot away from the next. The Romans came to this country to plunder its minerals. Here at Chester copper from the Great Orme at Llandudno, and lead from Holywell, could have been shipped back to Rome from Chester quite easily.

They called this fortress Deva Castra (Castle on the Dee) from the River Dee. I believe the name Dee comes from an old Celtic word meaning magical, special or mysterious. You will find many other opinions as to how the river got its name, but after years of research, this one appeals to me most, because of its Welsh connotations and the fact that the river does rise at the overflow of Lake Bala.

The Arms of the City of Chester taken from a 1905 postcard.

Shoemakers Row, 1890.

It is said that the English tribes moved into North Wales when Lancashire and Yorkshire were invaded in pre-Roman times and again in Saxon times, and that the only true English are to be found in North Wales.

There are some excellent books on Roman Chester as well as leaflets and pamphlets in the Grosvenor Museum. These set out life in Roman Chester and the formation of the city. One book in particular I found especially detailed and interesting; this was Curious Chester by Gordon Emery and I can recommend it.

The departure of the Romans is as murky as their arrival, but it was around AD 400. Certainly the 20th Legion, the famed Valeria Victrix, had moved out by AD 390, and by AD 418 Chester had been abandoned.

I have a theory that many of the Roman soldiers did not return to Rome, but melted quietly away into the Cheshire countryside. They knew that Rome was in trouble, they had not been paid for some time, and many of them had been at Chester so long they had wives and children here. So going back to Rome would have held little appeal to many of the soldiers. If the choices were to walk back to Rome and probably get killed, or snuggle up in the Cheshire countryside, which would you take? Cheshire and Lancashire have more Roman customs hidden in their folklore than Italy does, and I believe this comes from the many soldiers who did stay on.

A busy Bridge Street, 1860.

Christianity then moved into the void left by the departure of the Romans, and Chester was again involved. St Germanus led the 'Hallelujah Victory' over the Picts at Mold in AD 429, and it was at this time that the first church of St Peter and St Paul was built on the site of our present cathedral. In AD 603 St Augustus met the Celtic bishops at Chester, to try and resolve their differences before the slaughter at Bangor-on-Dee.

Chester was occupied, first by locals known now as Romano-British, then by the Saxons and for a few years by the Danes. Luckily it was restored to the Saxons by Ethelfleda, daughter of Alfred the Great, who married the Earl of Mercia. It was she who rebuilt the walls, realigned some of them and turned Cestre (Chester) into a fortified town once more. King Edgar was declared King of Britain here on the River Dee in AD 973. The next step in history was the coming of the Normans.

When the Normans invaded, Chester was the last of the English towns to give in. It was a De Trafford from Manchester who laid siege to the town in 1069 and because Chester was so important, with its 'gateway to Wales', that William the Conqueror gave it to Hugh Lupus. He was created 1st Earl of Chester and there were seven of them before Henry III took the title away from them and gave it to his son. Today the title is one of the Prince of Wales's: he is Duke of Cornwall, Earl of March, Earl of Chester, etc.

Hugh came over as Hugh d'Avranches but as his emblem was a wolf (Latin: *lupus*) he mounted his wolf emblem everywhere he ruled. He had land in twenty other places, including back in Normandy. He soon became 'Hugh the Wolf'. He kept his own Parliament and made his own laws. He hunted and killed wherever he wanted and caused havoc by taking whatever he fancied. The Welsh, who have a reputation for straight talking, called him 'Hugh the Fat' (Hugh Vras) and in their history they say that he was killed in 1100 in a battle near Abergele. Official history has it that he was so overcome with self-hatred and loathing that he gave up everything and entered the monastery of St Werburgh in Chester as a monk shortly before he died.

Over the years Chester has been at the forefront of the history of England. It was the last English town to fall to the Normans, and was under siege for two years during the Civil War (1644–6). Chester was the major port for the north-west of England from Norman times to the Middle Ages. The County of Cheshire was the strongest of all the counties and the first to be declared a 'Palatine' County, which meant that they could raise an army without permission from Parliament. They could also make and enforce new laws without royal approval and most importantly they could hold their own Parliament. Cheshire obtained this authority in 1330 and Chester was granted independence from Cheshire in 1506 by Henry VII.

There has also been a very strong connection between Chester and royalty over the last 1,500 years, starting with Saxon King Edgar in AD 971, who is said to have been rowed

down the River Dee by eight British chieftains to show that he was 'supreme, and over them'. Edward I used Chester as his base before constructing a string of castles at Flint, Rhuddlan, Conway and elsewhere, to keep the Welsh in their place.

It was to Chester that Richard II was taken after the takeover by Henry of Lancaster in 1399 and Henry VI held court here in 1459, as did his son Henry VII in July 1494. Charles I stayed here in August and September 1642 after the outbreak of the Civil War. James II was in Chester in 1687 and William Prince of Orange also visited Chester a few years later. Chester was once the cathedral seat for the large See of Lichfield, and also had its own mint for 'Cheshire coinage'.

The Grosvenor family have done much to give the city a helping hand. Not least is Grosvenor Park, given by the Marquis of Westminster in November 1867. It was in Victorian times that most of Chester's famous gates were rebuilt and the city walls put back in order. Chester knew the value of tourism as soon as the railway arrived in the 1840s. Stopping over in Chester for a few days to sample its delights, to see the walls, to walk by the river, became a must for the upper-class traveller, a habit soon copied by the middle classes and others on the move. The street lights arrived in Chester in 1899 and the city opened its first swimming pool and baths in 1900. The corporation was determined that they would be as good as any other city in the north-west, and they were.

The end of the nineteenth century saw a prosperous Chester, strong and busy; it saw the city ready to face the challenge of the newly emerging automobile and the coming Edwardian era. Chester was ready for the twentieth century.

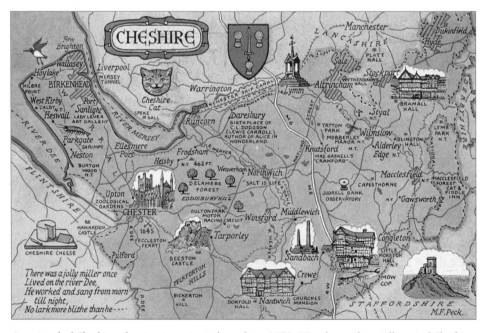

A postcard of Cheshire, showing important places from 1970. Wirral was then still part of Cheshire. (*J. Salmon postcards*)

Advertisements from a Cheshire Handbook, 1899.

A rare view of the Eastgate before the addition of the Queen Victoria Jubilee Clock. *c.* 1870.

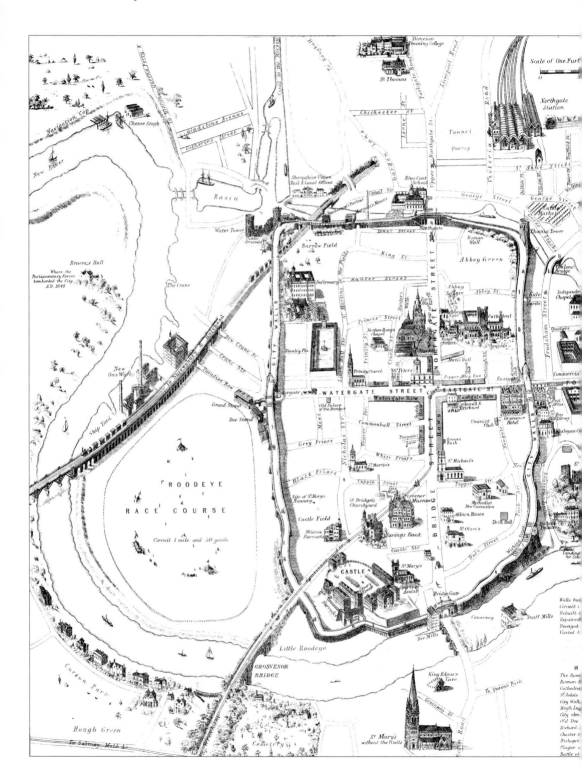

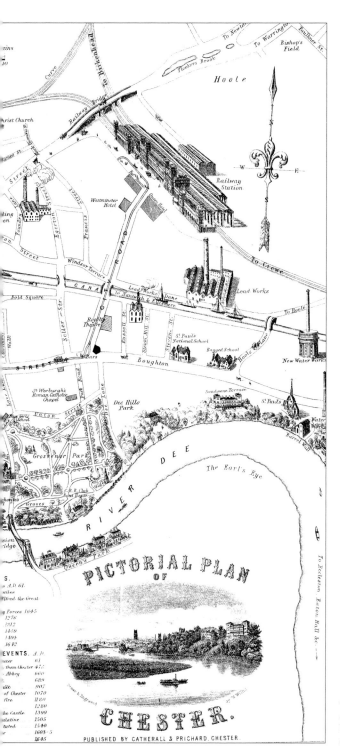

Chester, *c.* 1900. The map is taken from the *Stranger's Handbook to Chester*, issued in 1899 by Catherall & Pritchard Ltd, Eastgate Row, Chester.

THE

GROSVENOR HOTEL,
CHESTER.

First-Class; situated in the centre of the City, close to the Cathedral, the Rows, the River, City Walls, and other objects of Interest.

Two Large Coffee Rooms, and Drawing Room,
FOR THE CONVENIENCE OF LADIES AND FAMILIES.

Commercial, Billiard, Smoking & Stock Rooms.

Open and Closed Carriages, and Posting in all its Branches.
The Hotel Porters and Omnibuses attend the Trains for the convenience of Visitors to the Hotel.
A NIGHT PORTER IN ATTENDANCE.

TARIFF TO BE HAD ON APPLICATION.
APPLY TO THE MANAGER.

TELEGRAMS—GROSVENOR HOTEL
TELEPHONE No. 36.

BOLLANDS'
CELEBRATED BOXES OF
FANCY CAKES,
FOR AFTERNOON TEA, WEDDING RECEPTIONS, &c.,
3/6 and 7/- PER BOX.
Including Postage, forwarded per return on receipt of remittance.
—o—
ILLUSTRATED CATALOGUES GRATIS.

BOLLANDS',
CHESTER,
Confectioners,
By Royal Warrant to the King.

WEDDING CAKES
as Supplied to the KING.

WEDDING CAKES from 21/-
ALL SIZES KEPT IN STOCK.
Cakes packed in Tin-lined Cases for abroad.

FIRST-CLASS
RESTAURANT.
Table d'Hôte, daily, from 12 to 7 p.m.,
3/- and 4/6.
TURTLE SOUP.
Private Rooms for Parties.

BOLLANDS' CAFÉ
AND
SMOKE ROOM,
COFFEE, WINES & SPIRITS.

LUNCHEON HAMPERS
For Boating and Racing Parties.

Fancy Boxes of Bonbons and Chocolate, for presents.
From 1/- to 2 Guineas and upwards

WEDDING RECEPTIONS.
BALL SUPPERS.
LUNCHEONS. DINNERS.
GARDEN PARTIES.
WAITERS. HIRE OF PLATE, &c.

R. BOLLAND & SONS, LTD.

Two adverts from the 1899 Guide Book.

Bridge Street *c.* 1880, and horse-drawn cabs wait for customers. Within a few years horse-drawn trams would be running down Bridge Street and the pace of change would accelerate.

Chester in 1900

Monday 1 January 1900 dawned on a Chester that was a prosperous and thriving city. It was mainly residential and made its living running the affairs of the surrounding county and looking after the thousands of visitors who came to see the fortified medieval town, with its two miles of Roman walls. Queen Victoria was still on the throne, after celebrating sixty years as monarch in 1897. She was eighty years old, her health was very much a talking point, and all the celebrations had contingency plans in case she died as the century closed. She was to last just over another year, dying on 22 January 1901.

Another talking point was the war in South Africa. January 1900 saw Ladysmith under siege, peace talks with the Boers and a great victory at Spion Kop. There was an influenza epidemic in the capital. It was estimated that about fifty people a day were dying of flu in January 1900, and there was a great shortage of nurses and beds. Gravediggers were working day and night, and undertakers were talking of a backlog of funerals. The flu did come north and affected Cheshire, but not with the same ferocity as in London.

The start of 1900 saw a sense of well-being, and how 'Great' Britain was. Chester had been declared a County Borough some years earlier, in 1888, and the Cheshire County Council held its first meeting in April 1889. Electric street lighting arrived in the city ten years later. The landed gentry and upper classes of Cheshire regarded Chester as their HQ, their gathering place. The Chester Races, held during the first week in May, were a must on every social calendar. The Cheshire Show, also held on the Roodee at that time, was a great social occasion, finished off with a ball. The Chester Regatta, every Whit Saturday, and the Head of the River Race, every March, provided extra sport for the residents and was another attraction for visitors. Cheshire Cheese Fairs were still being held and Chester in 1900 was a very pleasant place to be. . . .

Looking up Bridge Street towards the Cross, *c.* 1885. The lines are down for the horse-dawn tram and there are still many local service firms with premises on the main city streets. Pearce, Watch & Clock Maker and Williams, Plumber, Glazier – and much else – are on the left.

Eastgate Street in 1900, showing the bank on the corner of St Werburgh Street. High-profile advertising was wheeling round a large sign for Maypole Tea at 1s 6d for half a pound – and I wonder why the horse-drawn delivery cart has Chester painted on the back?

A 1908 postcard looking up St Werburgh Street. The Cathedral is visible at the top of the street.

St Werburgh Street, but this time in about 1918. How quiet the street looks here compared with the nightmare of today's traffic.

Another ten years on and we see St Werburgh Street, complete with a new-fangled motor car, and how it looked at the time of the First World War (1914–18). By this time the street had been converted to cafés and coffee shops serving visitors to the Cathedral.

Northgate Street, *c.* 1905. This postcard was printed in Berlin. We are looking away from the Cross and Eastgate towards the Town Hall. The Rows, on the left, are a step up from the street, but not high enough for another shop underneath. Maybe it was built this way to give the better-class shoppers some protection from the muddy city streets. This row was Shoemakers Row, built in 1897 to replace an older street of two-tier shops.

Watergate Street, looking down from the Cross with Rows on both sides. Linen Market Row was on the left and the substantial Rows on the right are a Victorian rebuild.

The left-hand side of Watergate Street, showing the Rows, the old houses and Bishop Lloyd's Palace, taken from a 1904 postcard printed in Prussia. What a long way to go to print a Chester postcard, but agents from Prussia and Germany constantly toured all the tourist spots in the British Isles looking for trade for their printing presses, which were very much in advance of English ones at the time.

A lovely busy scene on Eastgate Street, *c.* 1902. I like all the street signs and advertising on display outside the shops – especially the optician's spectacles on the left.

Northgate, *c.* 1900. This is an unusual view looking across from the Town Hall steps towards St Werburgh Street and the Cathedral entrance. It shows how near the cathedral is to the Town Hall and the centre of the city.

Taken from the same vantage point as above but looking the other way across Northgate Street. Chester Town Hall dominates the centre of our photograph but the old Market Hall, complete with clock and statue, is to the left of our view. The Town Hall, seen here in *c.* 1906, was opened in October 1869 by the Prince of Wales, later Edward VII. It replaced the earlier Town Hall that burnt down in 1862. There was another large fire in 1899 which did a lot of damage to the Council Chamber, including damage to works of art.

The square outside the Market Hall and our postcard calls it Market Square, Chester, though the far side of the road is Northgate Street, *c.* 1912. The Cathedral, the Town Hall and the Market Hall are all just out of view.

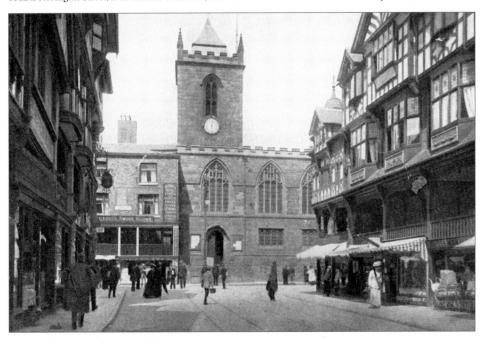

The Cross, top of Bridge Street. Although at the time there was no cross here, the area still retained its name. The first cross with its religious figures in niches at the top was pulled down and broken after the siege of Chester in 1643. The base and a stub of the shaft remained in place for about sixty years. In 1806 a new cross was made and re-erected at Netherleigh House. The original base and stump was presented to the Misses Butler and Ponsonby (the Ladies of Llangollen) in around 1817 and can still be seen in the garden at Plas Newydd, Llangollen. The reconstructed cross was moved to the Roman Garden in 1949 then back here in 1975.

Foregate Street, *c.* 1912. Correctly speaking only the left of the picture shows Foregate Street, up to St John Street. The rest of the photograph, from the Blossoms, right, is Eastgate Street. The Blossoms Hotel, established in 1650, had been completely rebuilt in 1896; in 1911, just before our photograph was taken, its frontage was pulled back to align with the rest of the street. Note the incursion of the motor car with Dee Motors, Agents for Rover and Flanders, having an outlet on Foregate Street, though it would have been more of a reception and spares area, the main works being on Bridge Street.

There is something I need to get off my chest and this is maybe the time to do it. I know that Chester has 'gates', archways and breaks in the city walls where people could enter or leave the city. The thing is that 'gate' in our street names today refers to an old, probably Anglo-Saxon, word, 'gata', meaning 'the way to'. In many northern towns they have accepted this and use the simple form, e.g. Deansgate, Micklegate, Fishergate, which crop up in Manchester, Leeds and Preston. York, another Roman town, has positively embraced these names: Watergate means the way to the water, and street comes from strata, meaning 'leads to', so the 'street' part is superfluous. If only the city council would bite the bullet and drop the 'street' in Eastgate, Foregate, Northgate and Watergate, then the city would have claimed back some of its roots. Bridge Street should be Bridgegate, and life would be so much simpler. Think about it please!

Opposite: Eastgate, 1910. The photographer must have been standing in Foregate Street to achieve this view. The two signs on the bank building on the left are, at the top, 'To St John's Church and River Dee' and the bottom one, 'St John Street'. The Hop Pole Hotel is on the very right of our fine Judges' postcard, and the garage sign on the right is where WHSmith's store is today.

The corner of Eastgate (right) and Bridge Street (left) known always as the Cross, *c.* 1910. Because of the black and white buildings and the unique steps, this view has always been popular with postcard manufacturers and here we see a view from the famous Judges' postcard series. The building on the extreme left of our photograph was built in 1888 when the Duke of Westminster demolished some of the property he owned in Chester that had fallen into disrepair, and had new buildings put up to match the style of the Rows, and in keeping with adjacent buildings.

Bridge Street, the west side, near the top of the street, *c.* 1900. Here we see four of the picturesque black and white buildings so evocative of Chester. It must have been half-day closing or early morning as there is little activity on the pavement. Clothes shops, ironmongers, drapers and rope makers occupied the buildings. Newman & Crittall the ironmongers had earlier been Powell Edwards & Co., plying the same trade. Thomas Cartwright at No. 10 (Compton House) was a hosier and R. Gregg was a rope and twine manufacturer. These buildings may be old and quaint, but they were successfully used as places of business and were busy commercial enterprises.

The Old Buildings

Within the city walls, Chester has many fine and very old buildings. The fact that many of them are in the black and white style that we associate with the Tudor period adds to their charm. This architecture helps to make Chester a very pleasant city to visit and adds interest to sight-seeing or shopping trips. Unfortunately, the mid- to late Victorian era saw much neglect of some of the older buildings. Many were past saving, but many were saved, and it was partly because of the Earl of Grosvenor (later the Duke of Westminster) that we have so many examples of these charming, eye-catching buildings still standing today.

Of course all towns and cities are constantly changing, and Chester is no exception. She has lost quite a few buildings that would have been a treat to see today, especially the old Market Hall. Many public houses became coffee shops and now some of them have changed into phone shops. Churches have been made into heritage and craft centres. There is nothing wrong in this. Buildings should be used, and it does add to the charm and the visible history of the city when lovely old buildings are restored and put to use instead of being demolished.It is nice to know a bit more about those black and white buildings and we cover those in the next few pages.

Looking down Watergate Street, from God's Providence House, on the left-hand side of the street.

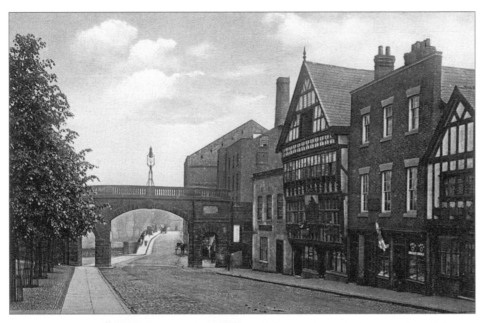

The bottom of Lower Bridge Street. Through the Bridgegate can be seen the old Dee Bridge which gives the street its name. Our view is from a postcard, printed in Prussia in about 1907. The large black and white building, third from the right, is captioned as the Bear & Billet, said to be named from the chained bear and ragged staff that was the emblem of the Warwick family (*billet* was the Norman French for a post or stave). In 1664 when the building was put up it was the town house of the Earls of Shrewsbury, the Talbot family. They were the Sergeants of the Bridge Gate and it was here that tolls were paid for entering Chester over the old bridge. Later it changed its name, but the Talbots continued to own it until 1867. The dark square above the windows are the folding doors of a granary where grain and provisions for the family were stored.

The black and white building on the far right is another inn, the King Edgar Tavern, named after the king who was rowed up the River Dee by eight princes to show their obligation to him. It was in a very poor state in early Victorian times and had recently been restored when this picture was taken.

A close-up of God's Providence House, complete with its row of chairs to sit and watch the world go by, as it looked a century ago.

God's Providence House, on Watergate Street, is sought out by visitors to Chester and is now one of the city's landmarks. Built in 1652 and restored in 1862 by James Harrison, it is said to be the one house not visited when the plague struck Chester. The only problem is that the worst plague to hit Chester was in 1647, five years before the house was built. The story could have been put about by a grateful person after 1648 when plague claimed over 2,000 Chester inhabitants. Since very early in the seventeenth century, Chester had been imposing quarantine conditions to try and avoid this Black Death. There had been plague in the 1360s which took roughly a third of the town's population. In the 1600s fairs were cancelled, people had to swear on the New Testament that they had not been to London and no London goods were allowed into Chester. It was 1657 before a coach ran to London.

Don't tell anyone but God's Providence . . . is also the motto of the Earl of Cork who passed through Chester a lot in the 1600s and it is on the front of houses elsewhere in England.

'Old House, Lower Bridge Street' is the caption on this late Victorian photograph. Built in 1603 the building was later known as Tudor House and is still there today, having been restored in 1907. On the right we see the building after restoration work. Cartwright, the Grocer & Provision Dealer, has been replaced by F.G. Quinn, who added baker to the previous services. The alley at the side was called Hawarden Castle Entry and the public house on the right was The Feathers, after the Prince of Wales's crest.

The Falcon Inn on Lower Bridge Street. Built in 1626 it was the town house of the Grosvenor family from nearby Eaton Hall. Many wealthy families had town houses on Lower Bridge Street in the seventeenth century. Like the Bear & Billet it became an inn and then the Grosvenors turned it into a coffee house in 1886 when it was restored.

Park Place and the Almshouses there, *c.* 1900. Originally there were nine of these seventeenth-century country-style dwellings and even though there are only six left standing the row is still called 'Nine Houses'. The large house nearest the camera was added in 1881 with the words 'The Fear of the Lord is a Fountain of Life' on its front. The words are said to be taken from a Roman coin found here. Park Place is often referred to as Park Street and is to be found inside the Newgate.

37

Stanley Palace, later Derby House, the town residence of the Stanley family, and (I am told) the Alderley (Edge) branch of the family. It was the Knowsley branch of the family who got the title Lord Derby so there seems to be some confusion in the story. Built by Peter Warburton when he was MP for Chester, the building's date of construction is given as 1591 – but surely that would make it older than the oldest house. It is on record as having been about 1700. As seen in our photograph above it was an antique shop for many years. It was given to the city by Lord Derby before being extensively restored in 1935. Since the Second World War the building has been the Chester branch of the English-speaking Union.

Between the Wars

The last winter of the First World War was a bad one, with a lot of harsh deep frost. There was some light relief to this bad weather in Chester though, with sports and skating organised on the River Dee just above the weir. Chester played an important part in the war; it was the Headquarters of Western Command, and much of the organisation of the war took place in Chester Castle. As peace descended and the country struggled to get back to normal, Chester's image as a tourist and holiday spot began to change. Many small industries sprang up, including paint and paper making and light engineering. Even with the great loss of young men during the war, jobs were still scarce. The tourist industry was greatly underfunded as resources went into agriculture, which was the mainstay of the area. The Cheshire Cheese Fairs and the Cattle and Swine Fairs helped pull the city around, though a meeting of the unemployed held on the Roodeye in 1921 echoed much of the frustrated feelings in the area.

The better-off, the upper classes, still had money, and that began to filter down in the late 1920s. Chester pulled itself back on to its feet. The Duke of Westminster helped with a rebuilding programme, which included the Queen's Park Suspension Bridge.

Eastgate in the 1920s, showing the Grosvenor Hotel and the Eastgate Clock. The hotel was built in 1865 on the orders of the Earl of Grosvenor. In the 1900s during Race Week the hotel would be taken over by the top owners and jockeys.

Eastgate looking down from the Cross, *c.* 1935. A lovely photograph – but how busy with traffic the street is. Up to the Second World War Chester let its traffic sort itself out, then as the 1940s drew to a close it started to make streets one-way, and the first signs of pedestrianisation appeared. I like all the shopping baskets here – even the bicycles had panniers and shopping carriers on them.

Note the Rows on the corner (left) of Eastgate are filled in and have windows on them.

Entertainments and Amusements.

It has become the policy of the Corporation during recent years to attract visitors to Chester by providing every facility for viewing and enjoying its ancient monuments. Each summer all buildings of interest are floodlit and the visitor can see old Chester in a new light. The illuminations by the river and in the Grosvenor Park, where music enhances the amenities, are particularly attractive.

Indoor amusements include six modern cinemas, a theatre, a news cinema, a greyhound racing track, and, during the winter season, ample opportunity for dancing.

Being within easy reach by road or rail of the Wirral Peninsula and the Cheshire hills, Chester is ideal as a residential as well as a holiday centre, and for those who work in the nearby industrial cities of Lancashire it provides a peaceful old-world atmosphere to which to return after a day spent amid the noise and bustle of modern commerce.

Eastgate and the clock on the gate at the end of the First World War. The Victoria Clock that dominates our photograph was given to the city to celebrate Queen Victoria's Jubilee. There were quite a few different schemes on the planning board and local solicitor Col. Edward Evans Lloyd wanted to speed things up. The Jubilee had been in 1897 and Chester had marked the occasion in style, but there was a danger of the Queen leaving this mortal coil before Chester put up its tribute to her. Lloyd agreed to pay for the clock. Douglas and Minshull, a local firm of architects, designed the frame and the clock. The frame was made by James Swindley, a local blacksmith, and the clock workings were made by James Joyce, the famous clockmaker from Whitchurch. The clock was officially started on Queen Victoria's 80th birthday on 27 May 1899 by the mayoress.

The Cross looking down Bridge Street, 1929. The tramlines are still there, but would be gone within twelve months. The building on the very right was erected in 1863 after an older shop on the site fell into disrepair. A lot of the left-hand side of Bridge Street was rebuilt then. The black and white building to the left of the corner had only been constructed in the later Victorian years (*c.* 1886) by the Duke of Westminster, but it was designed to blend in perfectly with the earlier buildings.

The same view as above, but there was a war between the two pictures. The card has a wartime message printed on the reverse and was used by 'VW' to tell her family that she had arrived safely back at camp at Ince.

Eastgate Street, *c.* 1935, complete with traffic policeman in his white coat on Northgate corner directing the increasing volume of traffic. It is just a trick of the camera and the angle the photograph is taken from, but it looks as if St Peter's Church has turned into the Victoria Hotel.

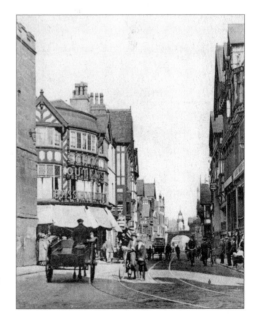

The School Outfitters and Boys Uniform Shop was a feature of Eastgate/Northgate corner for many, many years. How many youngsters have stood in that shop while their mothers have bought new shorts for school, longing for a pair of 'long' trousers so that they could be grown up?

Looking up Bridge Street in the mid-1930s. How much traffic there was. At the top of the street you can see one of the early buses that took over from the trams. The left is much older than the right side of the street, and of course the Edwardian shopping arcade, built in 1911 for the 2nd Duke of Westminster, is behind those buildings on the right.

A closer view of the Rows on Bridge Street, set into the black and white houses at the top of the street, *c.* 1930. That line of vehicles in the centre of the road are taxis, waiting to take the well-to-do home with their shopping from Chester's very upmarket shops.

Chester has been lucky with the support it has had from many wealthy local families, including the Grosvenors. When the private iron bridge, built in 1852, needed replacing in about 1920 money was soon found. The original bridge was built by James Dredge and was not for the use of the general public. When Queen's Park was planned as a development of houses, not a public park, then access to the houses was needed and the private bridge was replaced by a public one. The bridge opened in 1923 and is seen here on a 1926 postcard.

A general view and composite postcard of the glories of Chester in 1937. All that visitors associate with Chester, the Eastgate Clock, the Cathedral, the Cross, are on what must have been a very popular postcard.

When you stand at the Cross today you need a little imagination to picture what has been on this very spot in times past. The Roman Praesidium, the centre of all life for the Roman conquerors, was here. The meeting of the four main ways out of the city was here. This is where you started your journey to Wales, Manchester, or to the river and on to Ireland or Europe. This was the centre of everything in the most important Roman city in England. This was the spot where Edward II set out to conquer the Welsh, to unite the island that he saw as 'one', as Great Britain! This is the Cross in about 1929 with a mixture of trams and cars on the street.

A lovely postcard of the Rows at Eastgate, 1930. The Rows have added greatly to Chester's appeal, as they are unique, and there are no definite answers as to why they evolved, save our inclement weather and muddy roads. It really is pleasant to wander along the Rows today, in the twenty-first century, knowing that since the Middle Ages people have done exactly the same thing.

A lovely, evocative view of the Rows from 1932. The Victoria Hotel is on the left in the background and St Peter's Church too can be seen in the background on this *Liverpool Daily Post* photograph.

The Town Hall, looking from the entrance to Chester Cathedral in St Werburgh Street. This town hall is a very imposing building. It was opened in 1869 by the Prince of Wales, later Edward VII. William Henry Lynn of Belfast was the architect of this 120ft long building with its 170ft tower. There is no clock in the tower because at the time there was a large clock on top of the Market Hall next door, and the council did not want two clocks facing the square.

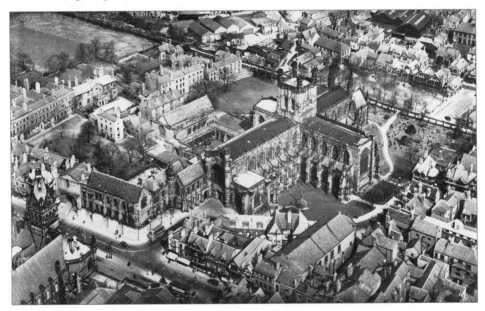

A lovely view from above Chester, *c.* 1930. The Cathedral dominates the centre of our picture, but the Town Hall can be made out on the very left. If you look at the middle bottom of the picture there is a lovely sandstone building with a very mixed history. Built in the fifteenth century it has been a chapel, music hall, a theatre and a cinema. The shop front was added in 1854 by the architect James Harrison.

Eastgate, taken from the gate itself, probably by a local individual, and turned into a postcard for him, 1929.

A lovely Francis Frith photograph of the Eastgate and the shops around it, 1929. WH Smith had opened their shop on the right and are still there today, though they have taken over the premises next door as well. The building on the right next to the Eastgate was Burton (the Tailors of Taste), and like many Burton shops put up in the north-west in the early 1920s had a café and reception rooms above it, designed to cater for weddings and funerals, and other local social events. The black and white building to the right of Burton's is only a few years old, having been built in 1921. At the time of our photograph the shop was Stewart's, another tailors. Most of Foregate Street, including the Blossoms, was rebuilt to realign the street, but they never got round to the building on the left.

Two views of the area around Eastgate, thirty years apart. The above view from *c.* 1905 shows a tram about to come through the 'gate' but it is the buildings on the right that we are interested in. The building next to the gate was soon to come down and be replaced by the Burton building seen below in the 1938 view. The middle building of these three on the right is in Chester's black and white style, but it is a garage. There is a lantern outside proclaiming 'Motor Garage', indicating that it caters for the new-fangled automobile. There was still an air of domesticity about this area in 1905, and many of the buildings and shops had people living above them. This practice had died out by the time of our bottom photograph. The third building had been revitalised and was WH Smith.

Eastgate, spring 1939. The Grosvenor Hotel is on the left and St Werburgh Street is hidden on the right. Our policeman directing traffic from St Werburgh Street has lost his white coat of the early 1930s.

Bridge Street in the months just before the Second World War. Chester may have lost its importance as a port, but it was chosen as the headquarters of the Western Command and was an important administrative centre throughout the war. The Castle was the centre of operations, but there were underground bunkers all round Chester, ready in case of invasion.

GROSVENOR HOTEL,
EASTGATE STREET, CHESTER.

There had been an old hostelry on this site known as the Royal Hotel. It was said that Charles I had eaten here, hence the name. In 1863 it was pulled down and the Marquis of Westminster paid for another hotel to be built to honour his father, Earl Grosvenor. It was designed and built by T.M. Penson, though he died before the hotel was completed. The hotel opened in 1866. Below we see an advertising postcard for the hotel and (right) the tariff for 1936.

List of Hotels, Boarding Houses, Apartments, etc.

LICENSED HOTELS AND INNS.

Abbrev. : B. & B.—Bed and Breakfast. G.—Garage. The number indicates the number of cars which can be accommodated.

NAME AND ADDRESS	BED-ROOMS	REMARKS
Grosvenor Hotel, Eastgate Street.	66	Centre of City. A.A.****. H. & c. water & telephones in all bedrooms. Bedrooms—12/6 single, 25/- double per night. Inc. terms p. w. 27/6. Ballroom, Grill Room. G. (80). Private suites. Tel. 1220-1-2.
Blossoms Hotel, Foregate Street	75	Centre of City. A.A.***, R.A.C. apptd. H. and c. water in all bedrms. Bed—single fr. 10/6, dble. fr. 21/- per night. Inc. weekly rate on appln. Billiards. G. (30) opp. Private sit. rms. Servants boarded. Tel. 186.

GROSVENOR

HOTEL

CHESTER

Tel. 1220

Chidley Photo

A composite view of the glories and special features of Chester in 1938. Eastgate and the Cross obviously feature, but the Cathedral, the Castle and the Grosvenor Bridge do get a look in.

The River Dee always was and always will be a great draw, *c.* 1920.

Looking up St Werburgh Street, *c.* 1935. The white-coated traffic officer looks as if he is getting a friendly word from his sergeant. Note the 'No Entry' sign hanging high on the left. The bus with its sign at the front is interesting; it looks as if it could be an early tourist bus for taking people round the city. It is seen coming up St Werburgh Street, which was always full of cafés and tea-shops for those visiting the Cathedral.

A very unusual view of St Werburgh Street, taken from the Cathedral and looking down towards Eastgate. The shop marked Hall's is today the SPCK (Christian) bookshop and does much to promote the Cathedral and Chester's heritage.

An advertisement for the Tamil Tea & Coffee Co. Ltd (below right) to promote the Tamil Café on St Werburgh Street (above). The lady peeping out of the doorway on the right has featured in many advertisements and books over the last seventy years. The very first espresso coffee bar of the 1960s was here in St Werburgh Street.

A clear and uncluttered St Werburgh Street, *c.* 1912. The way to St Werburgh's tomb is the best way to think of this street. It is not one of the original Roman streets, as it was not mentioned until the Middle Ages.

UNDER *the shadow of the Cathedral, and taking its place in the long story of the City, there is to be found and visited the source of the best coffee in the North of England*

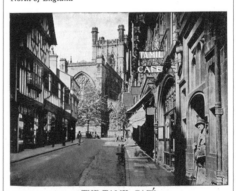

THE TAMIL CAFÉ
is proud of the value it gives and of the quality it serves

American, French, Swedish, and other visitors have all complimented the Tamil Café as being the one place where they have been able to get "a good cup of coffee"

THE
TAMIL TEA & COFFEE Co. Ltd.,
4 St. Werburgh St.   Tel. No. 608.

Abbeys, Priories, Cathedrals & Churches

When the Romans arrived at Deva, they would have had with them early Christians. The Christians would have set about making a place of worship and it is fairly certain that the first church they built was where the Cathedral is now, and was dedicated to St Peter and St Paul. The official Roman religion at the time was Mithraism, and they would have set up their altars and places of worship along the river bank. The body of St Werburgh was brought to Chester to keep it safe from the invading Danes in about AD 700.

There was a church here of secular canons founded by Ethelfleda, daughter of Alfred the Great, and this contained the shrine to St Werburgh, daughter of Wulfere, King of Mercia in the 600s.

The Cathedral was rebuilt by the Earl of Chester. Hugh Lupus, in 1093. This nephew of William the Conqueror came and rebuilt much of the city and put Benedictine monks into the monastery. This became St Werburgh Abbey and it is this building that we now refer to as Chester Cathedral. St Oswald's is the parish church attached to the Abbey.

St John's was the Cathedral for the district of Lichfield in the eleventh century.

St Peter's was mentioned in Domesday Book, as were other churches: St Mary's on the Hill, The Holy and Undivided Trinity, St Michael's, St Bridget's, St Olave's, all built by the Norman Earl of Chester and all twelfth century. Three Orders of Friars in and around Chester were: the Franciscans or Grey Friars, the Dominicans or Black Friars (near the Port Watergate), the Carmelites or White Friars. All disappeared when the monasteries were dissolved, but they are remembered in the street names of the city.

The crypt under Chester Cathedral, built in the twelfth century and used for storing supplies by the monks. This photograph shows it as it was in about 1920, with bits of the Cathedral stored ready for restoration. Today the crypt is used as the Visitors' Centre.

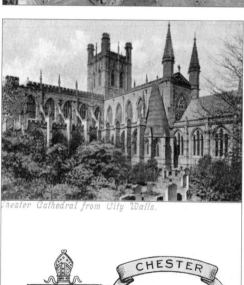

A very popular postcard of Chester Cathedral looking at the graveyard from the city walls, *c.* 1912. Also included are the Arms of the City of Chester and the badge of the Bishop of Chester with its four Bishops' Mitres.

The Cloisters and Chester Cathedral, *c.* 1910. The walls are ivy covered and there is an air of tranquillity about the old building. St Anselm's Chapel is on the left-hand side.

Saint Werburgh lived in the seventh Century. She was the daughter of Wulfere, King of Mercia, the great central kingdom of Saxon England, and became a nun at Ely. Later she was made supervisor of all the religious houses for women in Mercia. In the picture she is habited as an Abbess. In her hand she holds the Cathedral of Chester, which grew up round her shrine. At her feet lies the crown she laid aside to embrace the religious life, while in the background is old Chester with its walls. Beside her are two wild geese reminiscent of a legend connected with her. Once when she was at Weedon in Northamptonshire—now on the L.M.S. main line from Chester to Euston—she found that the wild geese were ravaging the garden. She summoned the geese to her and lectured them on their misbehaviour. Next morning they were worse than ever, and when S. Werburgh rebuked them, complained, "Yesterday, when we felt tame and good your cook caught two of us and made them into a pie." S. Werburgh agreed that this was not fair. She sent for the pie and the cook and they prayed, till at last the geese came back to life. Thereafter peace reigned, for both sides kept the peace.

Friend and pilgrim, take from S. Werburgh's shrine the motto, "Live and let live."

Visits to the shrine of S. Werburgh were very effective for healing all manner of ills. Then, as now, Faith was a mighty power. It is our lack of faith that makes us such impotent Christians.

Almighty God, grant to us, through the commemoration of thy holy servant, Werburgh, that honouring the purity and strength with which thou didst invest her, we may receive power to hallow and subdue both body and soul to the purposes of Thy Will; through Jesus Christ our Lord. Amen.

Early pilgrims to St Werburgh's shrine would have worn little badges to show that they had been there. Later visitors took away cards like the one reproduced above from 1910. St Werburgh was, by 1900, adopted as the patron saint of Chester and of Cheshire, and churches dedicated to her had sprung up all over the county.

This unusual card was published by Bamford's of New York. It shows the gateway to the Abbey Yard and yet has the simple caption 'Gate, Chester' leading one to believe it could be one of the original Roman gateways. It is certainly the size and style of one of those early gateways, far more than the now well-known Eastgate and Bridgegate. The niches on each side of the gate would at one time have held statues, especially one of St Christopher, whose face it was thought lucky to gaze on before starting out on journeys.

The cloisters of Chester Cathedral, 1938. Although we regard them now as just passages, they were the monks' meeting places and areas for taking exercise while in quiet prayer.

Chester Cathedral, S.E.

The Cathedral from the south-east. We see the graveyard and the large south transept on the left. The graveyard has been cleared away, though the gravestones have been preserved. The same view today is seen on the photograph on the right: the area is a well-kept and beautiful Garden of Remembrance. Both photographs are taken from the walls.

St Anselm's Chapel, *c.* 1940. The photograph shows the fine and ornate ceiling added in the early 1600s by Bishop Bridgman, who also added a screen and altar rails to this chapel. Charles I is said to have admired this ceiling when he stayed in Chester in 1642. Its nave was built in the twelfth century at the same time as the undercroft and the cellars below.

A 1903 postcard showing the famous Lector's Pulpit in the Refectory at Chester Cathedral. A lot of abbeys had pulpits in the dining rooms so that the monks could be read or preached to while they were eating their meals, not losing a moment for learning. The Refectory was built in the thirteenth century by Abbot Simon de Whitchurch, at the same time as the Chapter House and St Anselm's Chapel. Abbot Whitchurch gave great assistance to Edward I in his campaign against the Welsh, and Edward would have dined here before going on to Wales. The room fell into much disrepair in the late 1920s but was restored and a new roof added just before the Second World War.

The windows were altered in the middle of the 1500s though, and give the hall a later look. Today this is the eating area for visitors to the Cathedral, but I do not think they provide a monk for preaching during afternoon teas.

A reflective card showing one of the clergy resting for a moment in the Cloister Gardens, *c.* 1905. This sunken area was dug in about 1283 as a reservoir for the monks. The water supply was pumped from Christleton 2½ away. This card was a souvenir of the Abbey, not a postcard, and on the back is a Gaelic prayer.

Another view of the Cloister Gardens, with water lilies, 1930s. The postcard refers to it as the Pool.

The Cobweb Picture. The Madonna and Child painted, it says, on a cobweb, and preserved in a small corner of the North Transept of Chester Cathedral.

The west door of the Cathedral and
St Werburgh Street, 1965. The King's School
building is on the left, and there is still plenty
of traffic, including buses, using St Werburgh
Street.

The west door of the Cathedral as it is today.
What we see here comes mostly from Sir Giles
Scott's rebuilding a century ago.

Two of the wonderful features inside Chester Cathedral. Above we see one of the marvellous mosaic panels running along the north side. They tell stories from the Bible and would have been used to instruct the youngsters at Sunday School.

On the right is St Werburgh's tomb as it is today. The small statue of the saint was added recently.

Chester has other churches as ancient as the Cathedral. One of these is St John's, mentioned in Domesday Book, which unfortunately is more famous for its ruins than for the church itself. The official title of this church is St John the Baptist Without Walls, 'Without', of course, as opposed to 'within'. Above we see the ruins of the east end of the church which was the Choir. The lofty tower here collapsed in the sixteenth century.

On the left is a postcard from about 1920, again showing the glories of the ruins, at the Choir end of the church. St John's was started by King Ethelred in AD 689 and the Bishop of Lichfield, Peter, moved his seat here in about 1102. The Bishop did not stay long, fearing attack from the Welsh, and was soon back in Lichfield.

The magnificent Norman-style entrance to St John's Church, rebuilt and restored after the tower seen on the right collapsed on Good Friday, 14 April 1881. The ruins from the tower are still in position next to this entrance.

Here we see some of the early stonework at the river side of St John's Church. Note the narrow loopholes cut into the stonework. Some historians do not believe that King Harold was killed at the battle of Hastings, but made his way to Chester where he spent the rest of his life as a monk in the grounds of St John's Church. Adding credence to this story is the fact that his queen came to live out her life peacefully in Chester after 1066 and visited St John's Church often.

A postcard taken from Grosvenor Park looking at the famous Choir Ruins, which include a coffin set high in the walls. These ruins once contained a house where Thomas de Quincy lived for a time.

An early carved coffin top that is one of many inside the church.

A closer view of what was once the high altar of St John's Church. The lovely red sandstone work makes these ruins a very popular tourist spot.

Every corner of this fascinating church is full of pieces of history and interesting objects. The church always seems to be open and welcoming and there are notices and signs telling visitors all about the things they are looking at. Of all the churches I visit regularly St John's must be one of my favourites. Above we see two of the early clergy chairs preserved there.

One of the glories of St John's Church is the beautiful stained glass window put in by the Grosvenor family to mark Queen Victoria's Jubilee in 1897. It depicts stories from Chester's history and is well worth going to see.

VICTORIA·DINING·ROOMS.

Transport of Delight

Chester was on the busy route from London to Ireland via Holyhead and therefore always a major stop in national transport. Because the stagecoach and toll roads system was based on the earlier Roman roads, Chester was always destined to be a major spoke in the wheel of British travel. It was a stopping place, a place to pause, to change direction, and a popular place to get your breath back in the hurly-burly of old-time travel. All the great travellers of history have rested and written about our fair city and life there.

The canal followed the roads, then the railway arrived in 1840, when the Chester & Birkenhead Railway commenced services. The need for freight traffic to and from the docks at Birkenhead had pushed this route forward and it was soon joined by the Chester & Crewe Railway. The first railway station was in Broom Street, but it was only temporary and the companies were obviously waiting for further developments. In 1844 parliamentary permission was given to the London North Western Railway Co. to build a line from Chester to Holyhead. This was a major step forward and would open up the important Irish traffic to the newly emerging railway.

The Chester & Holyhead line had opened in 1846, and travel by train was now possible from London to Holyhead and onward to Ireland. This took days off the old style of mail coach travel, and when the Chester to Manchester line opened in 1860 the rail system into Chester General Railway station was more or less complete. The Chester station really is the hub of a transport wheel with spokes going out to Warrington, Crewe, Birkenhead, Llandudno and Shrewsbury.

The LNWR ran the station but its general manager in those early days, Captain Mark Huish, was very aggressive when it came to other railway lines. He had been known to pull one or two underhand tricks against companies that tried to encroach on his territory, and bought out small companies which stood up to the LNWR. This gave Chester General an air of conflict and there are stories of other company clerks being thrown on to the pavement, complete with tickets. Huish came up against the Shrewsbury & Chester Railway, and rather than buckle under, they fought back with the tenacity of a tiger rather than a Cheshire Cat. They brought in the Great Western Railway to back them and promised a through line from Shrewsbury to Birkenhead in return for their support. That put in place two of the strange workings through Chester. The line to Birkenhead was GWR territory and the line to Holyhead was LMS.

Opposite: The Church of St Peter at the Cross, *c.* 1880. The church was started by the Mercian princess Ethelfleda, who built a church here to take the place of St Peter and St Paul's (the Cathedral today) when its dedication was changed to St Werburgh's. St Peter's is built on the site of the Roman Praetorium and is one of the oldest churches in the Chester Diocese. The church is recorded in Domesday Book, and was the centre of the Chester Fair for many years in the Middle Ages. A glove would be hung outside for the fourteen days before the fair opened to show pardon for all who came to the gathering. Chester fairs were held in July and October, and there was also a 'Horn and Hoof Fair' when non-Freemen of Chester were allowed to come within the walls and trade.

Three views of the engines in the railway station from 1931. It was always a fascinating station with its mix of LMS and GWR, and in the summer the heavy excursion traffic from Yorkshire and the Midlands. Side tank engine no. 6703 waits in a bay platform at Chester General on a local stopping train in 1931.

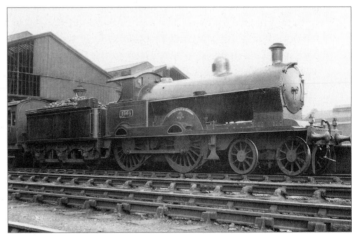

'Clyde' engine no. 1364 (later LMS 5258) has just pulled into Chester General with a north-west express in the late 1920s.

It was because of earlier feuds and take-overs that the LMS ran the line to Holyhead and Wales, and not the GWR as you would expect. As a result LMS engines stayed on the expresses to run onward to the Holiday Coast. Here we see 5343 'Otterhound' at Chester General in 1931 waiting to leave, probably for Llandudno.

The mixture of companies at Chester made it a mecca for trainspotters (including me). Above we see one of the Stanier LMS workhorses, 44687, in August 1961 with an express from Manchester.

'Black Five' 4–6–0s handled at least 50 per cent of the excursion traffic on the Resort Line to and from Chester. This is 45353 in November 1966 waiting for onward passage to the coast.

Because of the earlier disputes the GWR and the LNWR (later the LMS) had separate good yards and engine sheds. The LNWR engine stable was originally at the triangle west of Chester General but moved to the east, next to the Chester–Crewe line when GWR arrived. Here are three views from that LMS motive power depot, shed code 6A.

Two LMS engines caught on camera on shed in 1931: 1150 and 6640 Jinty locos in their pre-nationalisation garb. *(Locofotos)*

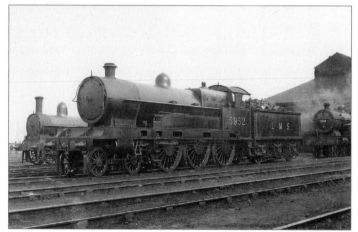

Engine 4–6–0 5952 waiting for its next turn of duty at Chester shed in the early 1930s.

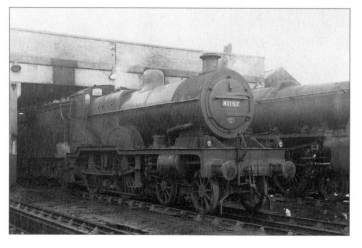

Chester shed in the late 1950s and 'Black Five' 41157 stands in steam on the motive power depot. The shed closed down in June 1967 and the site is now houses.

74

The GWR motive power depot at Chester was in the triangle west of the station, where the DMUs are kept today. Unfortunately, you couldn't make out the numbers from the station platform and had to make the mile-plus journey out of the station and across the bridge to get near the shed. The shed number was 84K and it usually had a few of the named classes on shed. Collett's 'Hall', 'Manor Grange' and even 'Castle' were shedded here in the late 1950s. Here we see two views from that GWR shed, above in August 1959, showing 6380 a GWR 2–6–0, and below side-tank 5647 steamed on shed and ready for a local train stopping at all stations. The GWR shed closed to steam in the mid-1960s but was retained for diesels.

Great Western engine 5038 'Morlais Castle' at Chester General station with an express destined for Paddington on 20 February 1960. The 4–6–0 Collett-designed engine had been built in about 1923, and the 127-ton loco and tender was ideal for these turns and nippy enough to negotiate some of the tighter bends on the line to Shrewsbury. Note the roof of the station had been partially taken away, soon to be replaced by 1960s umbrella-style awning. *(Locofotos)*

6976 'Graythwaite Hall' stands waiting for the all-clear at Chester General on 6 November 1960. The train was a Birkenhead to Paddington express and was usually brought from Birkenhead by two tank or smaller engines, then handed over. 6976 was a 'Modified Hall', built in 1944 and introduced towards the end of the war to help Britain back on to its feet. *(Locofotos)*

Chester racecourse was a great backdrop to trains leaving on the Wrexham line and passengers could watch the racing if the train was waiting to enter the station. Here we see 6337, a 2–6–0 engine introduced in 1911, on a Wrexham train, stopping at all stations, in 1949.

Same day, same situation, and a Great Western saddletank heads back to shed or station across the viaduct over the River Dee.

LMS locomotive 46127 Royal Scot class 'Old Contemptibles' leaving Chester on the Crewe line. Chester no. 2 signal box is seen behind the engine. The Royal Scots were first introduced in 1927 by LMS but rebuilt in 1943 with the taper boilers and distinctive smoke deflectors (plates).

With the smoke deflectors and taper boiler it looks like a Royal Scot but the engine seen here is one of the 15 Patriot class that were rebuilt in 1946. LMS No. 45529 'Stephenson' is named after George Stephenson, the man who did so much to establish railways. *(Locofotos)*

Jubilee class 45604 'Ceylon' LMS express engine, built in 1934, makes her way towards Chester General in the late 1950s, with a holiday excursion. The building on the right is the railway shed for Chester Northgate station built by the Cheshire Lines Committee, and now the site of Northgate Arena. *(Locofotos)*

Two LMS 'Black Fives' (44707 and 45047) in charge of a very heavy holiday special at Saughton junction on 21 June 1959. They will run straight through Chester General not stopping; first stop could be Prestatyn or even Llandudno. *(Locofotos)*

VIEW OF RAILWAY, ROAD, AND CANAL FROM THE WALLS, CHESTER.

A lovely postcard produced by the LNWR, *c.* 1905. It shows the railway and the canal, taken from the walls, near Pemberton's Parlour.

There was another railway station in Chester which seems to be forgotten today. It was called Liverpool Road station and was built by the Great Central Railway for the Cheshire Lines Committee out of Northgate. Here we see a good view of the station as it appeared in 1937 with its waiting rooms and ticket office, while below we see the station in 1959, closed and with its platform growing weeds. The railway line is still there today though it is used mainly for freight trains that want to bypass Chester.

Chester had a tram system, but really there was only one route, and the line ran from Chester General Railway station out to Saltney. It ran down Foregate Street, Eastgate Street, Bridge Street, Grosvenor Street and over the Bridge. The horse-drawn Chester Tramway Company was formed in 1878 and the line opened on 21 June 1879. It was electrified in 1903, taken over by the council and ran a useful service. The tram system was on a narrower gauge than those of most other major cities because of the narrowness of the streets. The route didn't last very long and had vanished by 1930. This is Eastgate Street, *c.* 1905, and an open-topped tram heading for the Cross. The line went into single file as it went under Eastgate.

A rare personal photograph of the trams in Eastgate Street in the late 1920s. Because the line was single in quite a few places during its journey through the city, drivers had to be patient and watch out for trams coming the other way.

Eastgate Street again and two trams taking the opportunity of passing before entering another single section. The scene is an Edwardian one. The electric tram system opened on 5 April 1903 and on opening day there were twelve trams, 23 ft long (numbered 1–12) to provide the service. Built by G.F. Milnes of Birkenhead, they seated twenty-three downstairs and twenty on top.

The Cross, Chester.

One of the twelve original open-topped electric trams rounding the Cross to head down Bridge Street in Edwardian times. Tram nos 1–12 were joined in 1905 by five more numbered 14–18 and these were built by the United Electric Car Company at Preston. All Chester's early trams carried forty-three passengers and were 25ft long.

The buses in Chester ran on two different levels and two different systems. There were local buses serving the local community. Then there was the excursion traffic, the buses heading to and from North Wales, the mecca of the holidaymaker from late Victorian times until the invention of the package holiday. Here we see Chester Corporation bus no. 5 on its way to Cliveden Road and Lache Lane just after the Second World War. The bus is a Guy double-decker and you may just be able to make out the famous 'Indian Chief' radiator cap, the Guy trademark for many years.

Much of the bus traffic was handled by two independent companies, the Crosville Motor Services and the North Western Road Car Co. These two handled the buses to the North Wales coast and into the Cheshire villages as well as Wirral, Manchester and Liverpool. Because of the width of some of the village roads, the lowness of some of the railway bridges, and the bridge crossing at Queensferry, many of the buses were single-deckers. Here we see two of the single-deck Crosville buses – the front one is a Leyland – waiting at Chester in about 1950.

A Crosville double-decker Bristol bus waits to leave on the 301 service to Llangollen, via Wrexham and Acrefair, passing through Australia. Yes, there is a place called Australia, just outside Llangollen. This was one of the busier Crosville services, which they took over in 1933 when they bought out Western Transport of Wrexham.

The original bus terminus was in Town Hall Square and here we see a bus enthusiast's photograph of two Chester Corporation buses loading in the square. The Corporation started their bus service in February 1930, just after a bill was introduced to end the tram service. The date is around 1962, just before the centre of Chester started to be pedestrianised and traffic restrictions tightened.

Crosville was a local company that had its base in Crane House and warehouse next to the Shropshire Union Canal in Chester. It was formed after Helsby man George Crosland-Taylor went to the Paris Motor Show in 1905 and became interested in the work of a French motor designer called Georges Ville. Crosland-Taylor purchased two sample cars in 1906 and shipped them to Chester; he also bought patterns, a chassis, and some parts, all to study. It was decided in 1908 to build cars in Chester to the French design and the Crosville Motor Co. Ltd was formed. It was soon decided that the premises were too small, and a larger modern assembly workshop was built across the access lane to Crane Wharf. There were only five cars built there and some had a wonderfully modern looking circular radiator. They also carried on general repairs and servicing on other motors and even converted a boat to run on motor power. In 1910, it was suggested that the company run a motorbus service to Ellesmere Port. To get between those two places you had to take the train and change, involving a delay, so after one or two hiccups the service started in January 1911 and Crosville Buses were on their way. The number of smaller companies they acquired was enormous: they took over roughly a hundred before the start of the Second World War. But they had also had the Great Western Railway buying shares in the company. Crosland-Taylor died in January 1923 and the firm was carried on by his sons W. James and Claude, though Claude died in March 1935. Crosville had depots at Liverpool, Bangor, Barmouth, Wrexham, Holyhead, Runcorn, Warrington and thirty others, but the home base was always Chester. George also founded the BICC works at Helsby and Prescott, called at the time the British Insulated and Helsby Cable Co.

The River Dee

Cities that have rivers running through them are lucky. Most ancient cities do because that's the reason that a settlement was started there. It's how they treat the river that seems to matter today. Liverpool loves the Mersey and they flourish together; Manchester seems to turn its back on the Irwell and the area struggles. Chester has embraced the Dee and Chester's riverside has been a source of pleasure and enjoyment for locals and visitors alike for over 1,000 years. The River Dee rises at Lake Bala or Llyn Tegid, in fact, the river is formed from the overflow from that lake. There is a folk story that a magical stream runs from the place that Merlin, the magician of King Arthur, is buried (near Y Parc) and the water is so special that it runs through Bala without mixing with the ordinary water of the lake; then it goes over the outflow and forms the River Dee. It is only a folk tale, but the Dee has many. There is no river in Britain that has so many stories and superstitions about it. When you see it thrashing through Llangollen or gliding past Bangor-on-Dee you get a sense of how special this river really is.

The Water Board don't seem to see it in the same light and it is the taking of thousands of gallons each day from the river that has led to the problems with the level at Chester and the trouble lower down the river at Parkgate and in North Wales. The word dee comes from a Celtic word meaning magical and mystical and that's what the river is, as we will see in the next few pages.

The old Dee Bridge, which gave its name to Bridge Street, seen here from the far side of the river on a postcard from *c.* 1930.

A lovely close-up view of the old Dee Bridge from a postcard, *c.* 1905. The mill at the bottom of Bridge Street is still there and you can also make out Bridgegate and the weir. In my opinion the water authorities take too much water out of the River Dee. Every day thousands of gallons are pumped away for industrial use. Water was taken out of the river for pop (mineral water) making, for sanitary uses, and by many industries for cleaning and washing. This mighty river does not have the amount of water that it once had, and should have. Until AD 132 the Dee Bridge was the only crossing of the river, and it was placed near where the Roman ford had once been.

A view of Chester and the Roodeye from Curzon Park with the River Dee running across the photograph. This part of the Dee is below the weir and therefore subject to the tide.

A really peaceful view of the River Dee from a card posted in 1907. At that time salmon were still coming up the river in large numbers and leaping salmon were still a feature of Chester's visitor attractions.

An early postcard of the Groves at the riverside, *c.* 1904. The weir was there and boating here was fairly safe, though the odd barge trying to get down river at high tide did come to grief or get into trouble at the weir.

A view of the Groves on the banks of the Dee as they looked a century ago. This is the river in the summer of 1902 and has the old suspension bridge in the background. The Edwardians did not mind a primitive feel to their excursions and it shows here.

The River Dee at Chester, over 100 years ago. The boats to take the visitors down to Eaton Hall were there and the weir kept the level of the Dee high and constant.

The Groves on the banks of the Dee, *c.* 1920. Boating had by then developed into an art form, every male trying to prove that he could handle a craft. Restaurants and cafés had sprung up along the river banks and the Groves were becoming more of a tourist attraction.

A postcard from just before the First World War of the Groves and the boats and other attractions.

These two pictures are roughly twenty years apart, yet they show how the river changed from being a pleasant aside to a very important cog in the tourist industry of the city. The 1851 suspension bridge in both pictures is, of course, the first bridge at this spot. The top photograph is from the summer of 1904 while the one below was taken in about 1924.

Workmen putting the finishing touches to the new Queen's Park Suspension Bridge early in 1923. The name is a little misleading because Queen's Park was not a public park; maybe it should have taken its name from the Groves or Grosvenor Park which is on this side of the river.

The old iron bridge which crosses the River Dee further upstream by Eaton Hall and Eccleston.

A rare and unusual view from the Groves looking over at Handbridge and St Mary's Church on the south side of the Dee. This photograph is from about 1900.

The city walls and the River Dee, with the Recorder's Steps, seen here on an Edwardian postcard.

The Walls

Chester is the only city in Europe that still has a complete wall surrounding the old city. These walls give enormous pleasure to the visitors and the people from the Chester area. To walk the 2 miles of the walls is a peaceful exercise in today's busy world. It has taken great efforts to keep these walls complete, but it has paid off handsomely. Over the last 250 years new gates have been built, missing parts of the wall replaced, and plenty of general upkeep has been required. Just how much of the walls that we see today are Roman is hard to determine, a point that is often brought up for discussion. Much of Roman Deva lies beneath the city, and that includes most of the original Roman wall, which is still being unearthed below the city streets. When Ethelfleda in the 900s came and rebuilt the city in the pre-Norman era, the walls were built tighter than the Roman walls, pulling in the defences. There was further refortification of the walls in the Tudor and Civil War period, from which some of the present towers date. The Eastgate with the large 1897 clock is the main entrance. King Charles's Tower is said to be where Charles I watched the defeat of his army by the Parliamentarians after the city had been besieged for two years. Watergate, on the west side, was once controlled by the Earls of Derby who charged a toll on goods taken into the city through this gateway; and in 1966 St Martin's Gate was built to allow the ring road to breach the walls. So it is that the walls we walk today are not the original Roman-built walls, but they do give us an idea, and the feeling of continuity down the centuries.

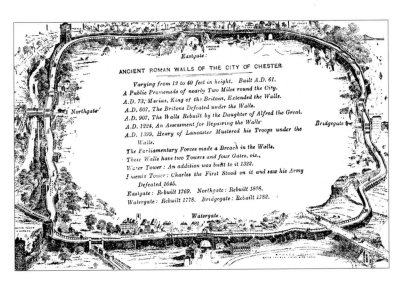

A 1905 postcard extolling the virtues of the Roman walls. This is what visitors of Edwardian times sent home when they visited Chester.

The names of the towers have changed over the years depending upon their use. Many were used by guilds and societies as meeting places and were known by the name of the society that met there. There were at one time no fewer than seventeen towers around the walls; all but four have been removed.

Above we see a postcard from 1906 showing the Water Tower and the Roman bath next to it from outside the walls. Below is the Water Tower from the more usual angle, but on the left it is marked Bonewaldesthorne's Tower. On the right the caption reads Water Tower. This is a 1906 postcard. This tower in early days was known as the New Tower and was a defensive position to guard the port and shipping which would anchor just below this spot. The tower was used as a museum for a time. The statue of Queen Anne in the bottom photographs has since been removed.

This is the Phoenix Tower. The Phoenix was the crest of the
Chester Guild of Painters and Stationers who used it for their
meetings. The rent was 2*s* per year in the early 1600s. After
24 September 1645, when Charles I watched the battle of Rowton
Moor and the defeat of his armies, it was always fated to be
connected with him and has been called the King Charles Tower
ever since. It is seen here in our picture from 1920 on the right.
This tower has part of the original fortifications in its structure. The
Phoenix of the painters can still be seen over
the doorway. This tower has also been the meeting place of
the Company of Joiners, the Butchers and the Weavers and
Clothworkers. The steps were added so that guild members could
attend their meetings without disturbing those meeting below.

A view of the city walls from the Dee Bridge area, late 1920s. The walls have always been part of the city's life and have been used for the city's business, defence and everyday life. We see here how the walls and the river provide a double defence for Chester.

A 1930s postcard showing the steps up to Bridgewater and the Groves beyond the walls.

People & Places

You cannot mention Chester without talking about Chester races. Horse racing here in the city was recorded well before anywhere else in England. In about 1524, the mayor of Chester decided that the 'footballe' played here was dangerous and would be replaced by horse racing. The Chester Cup has been raced since 1824 and the May Meeting is more than 250 years old. Recently other meetings have been added to the calendar, but the main attraction is still the first Tuesday, Wednesday and Thursday in May.

As a small boy I would go to the races with my Mum on the H2 Crosville bus from Widnes to Chester, to be joined at 1 p.m. by my Dad, who had shut his barber's shop early. Aged only seven, I had a win on a horse called Papa Fourways at 10–1 with a half-crown bet given by an uncle. My Dad held my winnings for me and I must have spent it ten times over.

Chester Races are just one of the many attractions of the city; another jewel in the crown. They kept the importance of the city as a meeting place early in the season and the start of May would see royalty staying with the Grosvenors, the Bromley-Davenports and the Leverhulmes, all gathered to attend the races. If you were anyone of importance you were in Chester the first week of May.

Chester Racecourse and the walls, which are very much part of the course, c. 1920. In the distance are private residences and the railway bridge which runs alongside the course.

A good vantage point for the general public from the Walls and Nuns Road, 1910. In the 1800s, there was no charge for admission to the races. A shilling was the admission charge in 1893. It always amazes me the way that postcards travel. This view was posted from Chester to Queensland, Australia, and presumably got there, but how did it get back to my collection here in England? I bought it at a postcard fair from a Wirral dealer, Ted Gerry.

A view of the Roodeye (Roodee) as it looked in 1890, before Nun's Road was made. Rood is an old word for Cross and eye was marshy land that is liable to flooding. There is just the base of the original cross left there today.

Chester Races have always been a flat race course, but now and again they held a point-to-point. Here we see a very rare photograph of a hurdle race for gentlemen riders, *c.* 1890. The stands shown here were erected in 1817 to a design by Mr Harrison, the County Architect, and replaced in 1899.

CHESTER, WEDNESDAY 9th MAY 1979

Ladbrokes Chester Cup
OFFICIAL PROGRAMME

BETTER BACK THE WINNER

⌐ Ladbrokes

An unusual view of the Roodee in the 1960s. Chester Racecourse is seen from the River Dee just at the side of the railway bridge. The Town Hall, St Peter's and Trinity Church (now the Guildhall) pierce the skyline behind the county stand on the right. This famous stand burnt down in 1985 and had to be replaced, though the new stand cost around £2.5m. and not the £12,500 of the original when it went up in 1899.

A rare view of King Edward VII leaving the stand at Chester Races, after enjoying a pleasant afternoon watching the horse racing, *c.* 1908.

The thrilling finish to the Chester Cup, at some point in the 1950s. Note the thousands in the crowd, and how the walls and banking were used as a natural stand.

The races at Chester were so popular that thousands turned up for them. In the years up to 1914 it was a race in itself to photograph the winner of the big races and produce a postcard to sell to the punters on their way home. From 1902 to 1914 there would have been portable photographic studios all around the Roodee. Here we see the finish of the Chester Cup in 1905 won, as it says, by 'I Man'.

The scene at Chester Town Hall and the crowded square outside, as the mayor of Chester proclaims Edward, Prince of Wales and Earl of Chester, as King Edward VII in 1901.

Chester Zoological Gardens were started by George Saul Mottershead in the early 1920s and carried on by his family after his death. They were taken over by the Zoological Society in the 1930s. Here we see the inside of the Zebra House, on a postcard from 1955.

A collage of the cinemas and theatres of Chester, taken from a council publication of the 1950s. One to note is the Music Hall Cinema, centre right, which started life as St Oswald's Church.

The castle at Chester, *c.* 1900. The castle has always been a military and administrative centre. There was a fortress here before the Norman conquest, and later the Barons of Chester held their Parliaments here. Part of the castle has Roman foundations, but it was the Normans who rebuilt it in about 1070. It was often used as headquarters for English kings when making war on the Welsh. It is still in use today as a Court of Justice and military museum.

The impressive entrance to Chester Castle, with the statue of Field Marshal Viscount Combermere (1773–1865) mounted on his horse. He sat and posed for it during the last two years of his life. Born Stapleton Cotton, he was 6th Baronet, and Provincial Grand Master of the Freemasons in Chester.

The Chester Band of Hope parades through the streets in 1913. This Band of Hope was a youngsters' organisation which pledged to do good deeds every day.

Ellesmere College, 1917. You can make out soldiers sitting on the benches watching a cricket match. The College is obviously being used as a military hospital or convalescent centre. This card was posted by Private R. Sherwood, to his friend Corp. McBurney, in a nursing home in Shropshire.

The interior of the old Stanley Palace, 1903. The kitchen had been re-created for visitors who paid 6*d* to go in and have a look around. Note the baby's cradle next to the fire.

The Bishop of Chester, Francis John Jayne, poses here on a 1906 postcard. He had held office since 1889.

Chester's past is very colourful and the historical pageant held every few years was always a big draw. On this postcard, from Edwardian times, we see a painting of the scene of the visit of James I to Chester in 1617.

A card from the Oilette series, showing the Bishop of Chester about to take his seat on the Cathedra.

An advertisement from the 1950s, offering shopping and sightseeing, as well as a holiday in Chester. The official Guidebook was priced at 1s 6d.

Right: A little bit of history caught in this newspaper from 23 August 1962. It tells, as you can see, of Ringo Starr joining the Beatles. It also states that the Beatles start a four-week engagement of Thursday nights at the Riverpark Ballroom, Chester, on 16 August 1962. This is thought to be the first time that the Beatles appeared in public with their new drummer. Russ Abbott played there with his group, the Black Abbots, for a time.

A 1960s advertisement.

Chester College, and its Elizabethan-style frontage, 1910. The College was started as the Chester Diocesan Training College in 1839, and this building opened in September 1842.

An Edwardian postcard of students enjoying a game of cricket on the recreation grounds of Chester College. The College trained teachers for public elementary schools.

Eaton Hall & the Grosvenor Family

The title Earl of Chester may have gone to the royal family but there were still descendants of Hugh Lupus and the Norman Earls. This family became the Grosvenors, and Queen Victoria raised Earl Grosvenor to the title Duke of Westminster, the only such event during her reign, as all the other Dukes made were members of the royal family.

Hugh Lupus Grosvenor was the 1st Duke of Westminster and was MP for Chester from January 1846. He made a good MP and his compassion showed in the bill he promoted concerning shop opening hours. When he inherited the title Marquis in 1869 almost £5 million came with it and an income of over £150,000 a year from rents. At the time income tax was 5*d* in the pound, and it decreased to 2*d* in 1875.

The original Eaton Hall, which stood just south of Chester, was built by William Samwell, a gentleman and architect, in about 1800. It was a fine house of classical proportions. The house was not big enough for the large Grosvenor family who moved in and in 1802 the 2nd Earl had it pulled down, commissioning William Porden to build a new house. Unfortunately, the new hall was described as 'a vast, hideous, cold and comfortless pile'. The interior was said to give 'little but chilly discomfort in tasteless splendour'. This house was pulled down by the 1st Duke just after his father's death in 1869, and he chose Alfred Waterhouse to design and build the new Eaton Hall. This is the hall that we see in our postcard selection over the next two pages. Waterhouse had made his name designing town halls, and his critics dubbed the house Eccleston Town Hall, as they said it looked more like a civic building than a house.

The Grosvenor family crest.

Waterhouse's Eaton Hall, seen here from the garden. It was an impressive building, though rather over-ornate. The 1st Duke had it built in 1870 and an extra private wing for the family was part of the design.

Eaton Hall from the front, showing the drive and the magnificent gates. Behind those seventeenth-century gates is a very fine statue of Hugh Lupus mounted on his horse, carved by Watts, but it is hard to make out. The clock tower is reminiscent of Manchester Town Hall's.

Eaton Hall from the River Dee showing the palatial steps. It was the marriage of Sir Thomas Grosvenor aged twenty to Mary Davis, heiress to the Ebury Farm Estate, which formed much of the city of Westminster. The names from around Eccleston (Street) transferred to one of the richest areas of London. Eaton (Square), Belgrave (a farm on the estate) and Grosvenor (Square) are all now part of London's history as well.

A drawing of Eaton Hall from the river, issued as a postcard in 1905 by the LNWR. The Hall as seen here was pulled down in 1961 by the present Duke's father. Only the clock tower and the chapel, which contain the first Duke's ashes, were retained. A modern, centrally heated, Eaton Hall stands there today. The Grosvenors are a good example of a family who take their duty to their workers seriously. In the Victorian era there were around 300 estate workers and farmhands on the home farm and other farms around the large estate.

Eccleston Ferry on the River Dee. It really was and still is a very popular place for a picnic, and a stopping place for the boats coming up river from the Groves in Chester. Eccleston was a village created by Earl Grosvenor who became the 1st Duke of Westminster. It is still a very interesting place to visit and explore. It has kept a lot of its original charm and looks very much as when it was first laid out by the Duke. It was he who planned and financed the church and built the houses for the estate workers. His monument is one of the glories of the church there. There are quite a few of the family buried there and many fine statues, busts and other memorabilia to them. I find the words on one family brass quoted from Christina Rossetti quite moving:

> Better by far you should forget and smile,
> Than that you should remember and be sad.

Chester Today

Most cities in Britain have had problems over the last twenty years with shops closing on high streets. Out-of-town shopping centres have taken business away, and Cheshire Oaks has tried to pull shoppers away from the Chester area. Chester seems to have handled the changes better than most places: it has survived much better than many other northern places. I think it's because of the number of upmarket and quality shops that it has, combined with its down-to-earth market. I take visitors on days out in the north-west and can say with hand on heart that you can guarantee a pleasant afternoon shopping or just eating in the city. The only criticism I have come across is that many of the shops close a little early, once the summer has finished. In today's markets, it would be nice to see a bit more life around the shops in October and November during tea-time and early evening. I know they have late shopping in December but maybe more shops could open late all year round. I know Chester has gone the way of many other high streets, and phone shops and charity shops are there in larger numbers than anyone could ever need. If they don't make money they will go away and be replaced. I remember thirty years ago complaining that there were too many building societies on the high streets.

Chester has so much to offer that it will always do well and always present a welcoming face, whether you are coming from Saltney or Singapore.

Italian street musicians provide colourful entertainment in Northgate, summer 2001.

The riverboat Princess Diana comes under the suspension bridge after another trip up the River Dee to Eccleston, July 2001. The boats have been here for as long as Chester has attracted visitors.

A peaceful scene down at the riverside with swans and their cygnets keeping an eye on the visitors and locals who enjoy this spot. It was Hugh Lupus, the first Norman Baron of Chester, who had the weir constructed so that water could be channelled off to a mill at the bottom of Lower Bridge Street.

Chester in the twenty-first century has charms
on many different fronts. One of these is
the mixture of shops and ancient buildings,
including inns and taverns. Above we see the
Blue Coat School, by Northgate, in 2001. It
was founded in 1700 by the Society for the
Promotion of Christian Knowledge (SPCK)
as a charity boarding school. A day school
was added in 1790 and closed in 1901.
The boarding school closed in 1949 and the
building is now used by the University College
as the history department.

St Peter's Alley behind the church, one of the
many ginnels that exist in Chester today.

Here we see St Michael's Row, which today is part of the Grosvenor Shopping Centre. This is Edwardian shopping at its very best, beautifully tiled and ornate, with a glass roof. Nothing could be added to this splended arcade, which adds style and comfort for shoppers and tourists.

The Rows at the Cross. One bonus that the Rows gives us is protection from the elements on wet and inclement days.

The Amphitheatre next to St John's Church. What we see here today is only part of what was the largest Roman amphitheatre in Europe. It was 189 x 161 ft and 62 ft deep, and could seat 10,000 spectators in twenty or more tiers of seats. Today they hold the Miracle Plays in this half-excavated area. The Miracle Plays date from 1422, and are performed every three years, and were last held here in the year 2000.

Most of the walls surrounding Chester are fairly uniform at 20-30ft high, but in places they have to be much higher. Here we see the highest part of the wall as it approaches the Groves and the River Dee. This picture gives us a sense of how imposing the old walls must have been.

Eastgate today. Work is constantly going on to keep these old buildings up to scratch. Here we see WHSmiths getting a face-lift.

St Werburgh Street, still mostly cafés and eateries, although one or two of the tea-rooms have now changed to delicatessens. This view is from summer 2001, and although shops have been changing their character, it is still a busy street.

The Falcon Inn, on the corner of Lower Bridge Street and Grosvenor Road. Built almost 400 years ago, this ancient tavern was restored in 1886 and turned into a Coffee House. It was restored again in 1982, when Grosvenor Road was widened, and has gone back to serving ale and porter.

The old black and white houses add wonderfully to the charm of Chester. Here we see God's Providence House on Watergate Street, in 2001.

Chester's General Railway station in 2001. The early Victorian architecture of this building deserves more recognition than it gets. The clock in this photograph was moved to face City Road so that early travellers could keep their eye on the time as they approached the station. Later the clock was moved back to its original site.

The Queen Hotel facing Chester General is still large and comfortable. This fine Victorian hotel was built for the wealthier and more discerning rail travellers. Today it offers a unique service for travellers in this part of Chester.

A stretch of the Shropshire Union Canal, 2001.

Looking from the Cathedral across the ancient courtyard towards the Abbey Gate. This gate is thought to be the size and shape of the original Roman gates.

One of the fine displays in Chester Cathedral's Visitors'
Centre. In what was once the crypt, the Cathedral has
opened a very informative centre which guides the
public through the history of this place of worship.

'A Celebration of Chester', situated in the square outside
Chester Town Hall. This fine modern sculpture, by
Stephen Broadbent, represents thanksgiving, protection
and industry.

Acknowledgements

Thanks are given to Gordon Coltas (*Locofotos*) for permission to use his fine collection of Chester steam train pictures, to Ted Gerry the postcard dealer for help with some of the rarer postcards and views, and to my wife Sylvia for her patience in typing and re-typing the manuscript. All unacknowledged photographs are from Cliff Hayes's collection.

Grosvenor Park today. The 2nd Duke's statue can just be seen at the end of the tree-lined walk.